2nd Edition

THE Beatles

PIANO DUETS

INTERMEDIATE LEVEL
1 PIANO, 4 HANDS

T0034021

ISBN-13: 978-0-7935-8338-6

HAL•LEONARD® CORPORATION
7777 W. BLUEMOUND RD. P.O. BOX 13819 MILWAUKEE, WI 53213

Visit Hal Leonard Online at
www.halleonard.com

CONTENTS

CAN'T BUY ME LOVE

SECONDO

Words and Music by JOHN LENNON
and PAUL McCARTNEY

CAN'T BUY ME LOVE

PRIMO

Words and Music by JOHN LENNON
and PAUL McCARTNEY

SECONDO

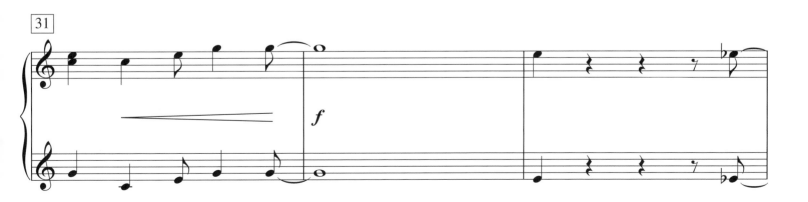

SECONDO

PRIMO

SECONDO

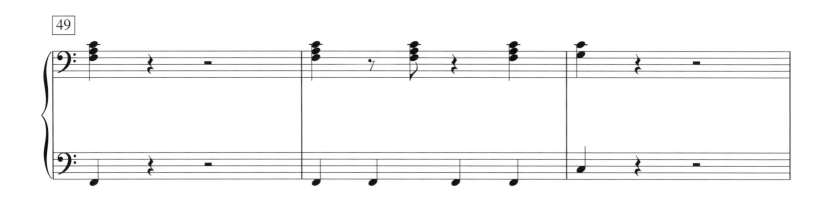

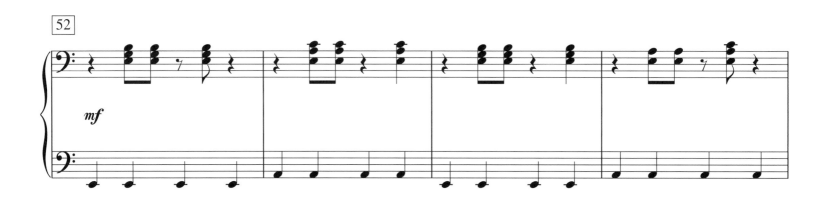

ELEANOR RIGBY

SECONDO

Words and Music by JOHN LENNON
and PAUL McCARTNEY

ELEANOR RIGBY

PRIMO

Words and Music by JOHN LENNON
and PAUL McCARTNEY

Moderately, with a steady beat

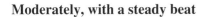

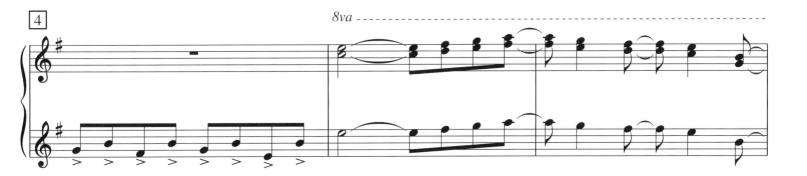

SECONDO

HEY JUDE

SECONDO

Words and Music by JOHN LENNON
and PAUL McCARTNEY

Moderately slow

HEY JUDE

PRIMO

Words and Music by JOHN LENNON
and PAUL McCARTNEY

Moderately slow

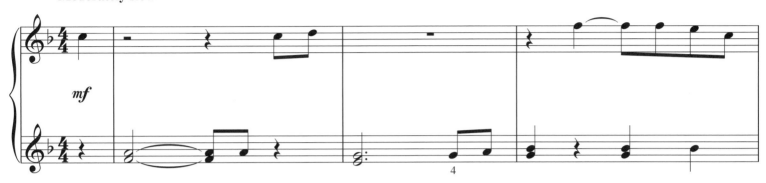

SECONDO

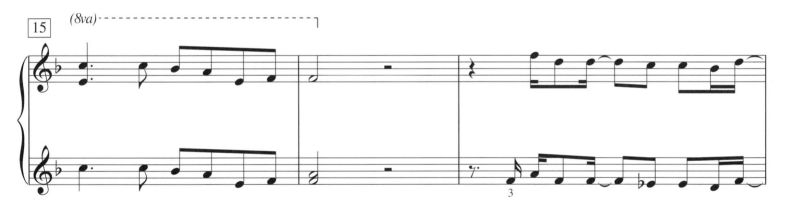

SECONDO

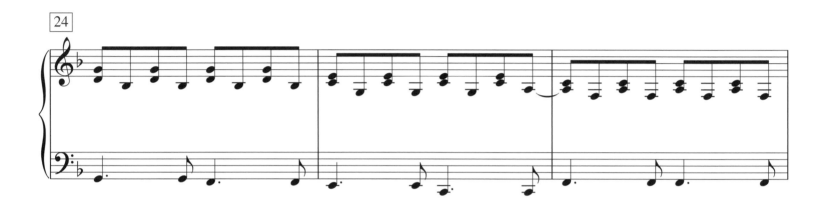

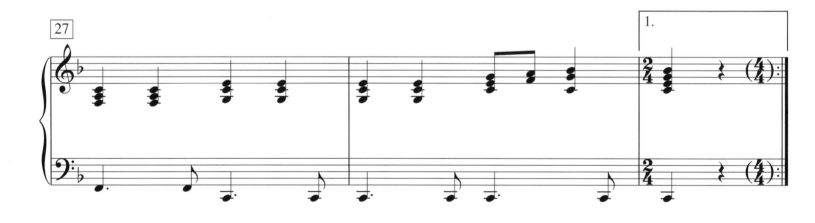

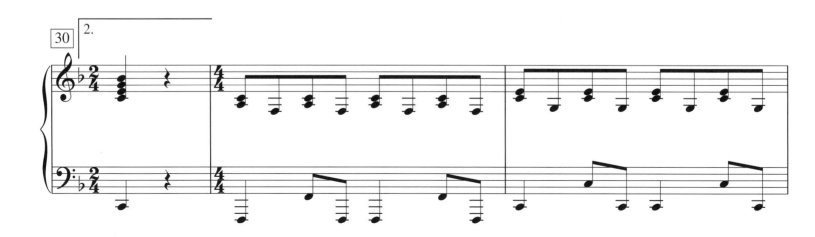

PRIMO

SECONDO

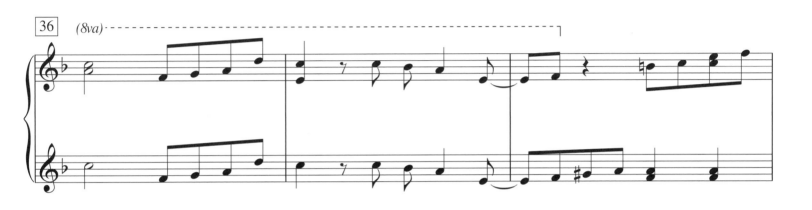

LET IT BE

SECONDO

Words and Music by JOHN LENNON
and PAUL McCARTNEY

Slowly

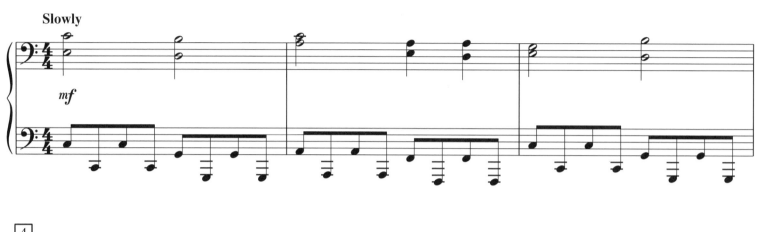

LET IT BE

PRIMO

Words and Music by JOHN LENNON
and PAUL McCARTNEY

SECONDO

PENNY LANE

SECONDO

Words and Music by JOHN LENNON
and PAUL McCARTNEY

Medium Swing

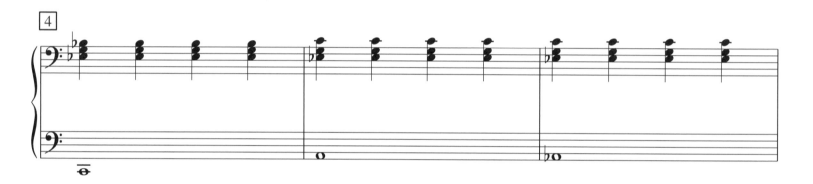

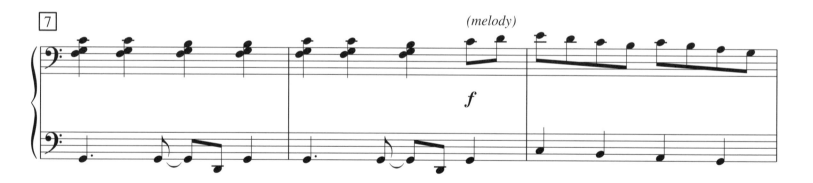

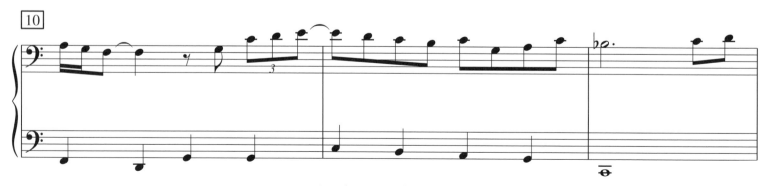

PENNY LANE

PRIMO

Words and Music by JOHN LENNON
and PAUL McCARTNEY

SECONDO

SOMETHING

SECONDO

Words and Music by
GEORGE HARRISON

SOMETHING

PRIMO

Words and Music by
GEORGE HARRISON

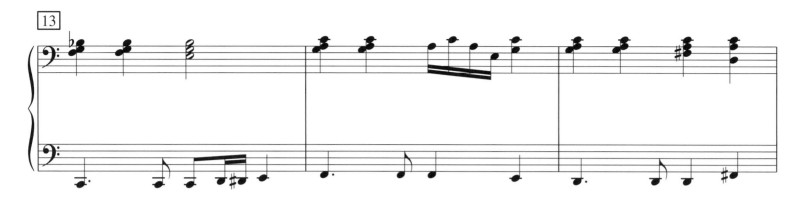

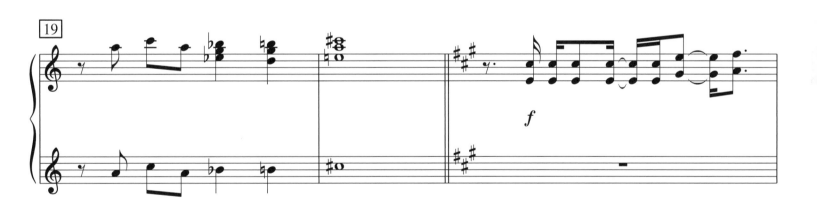

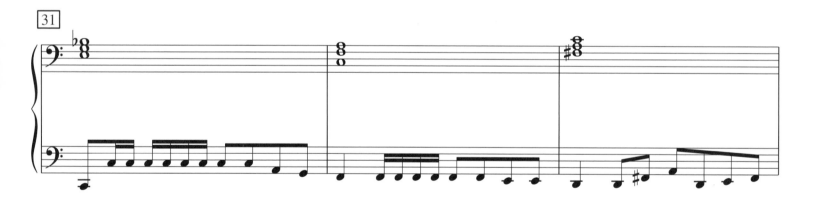

SECONDO

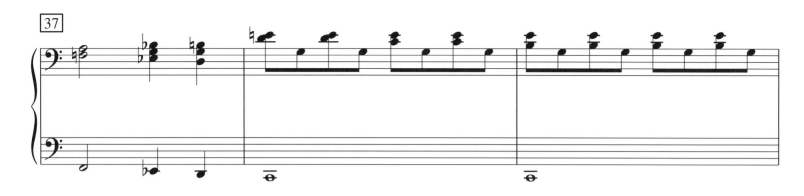

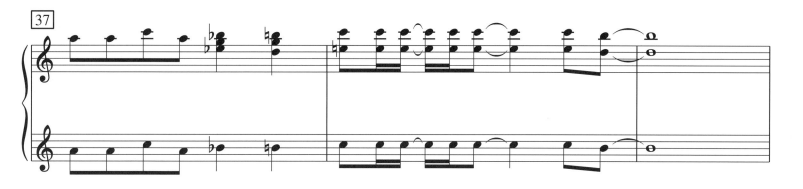

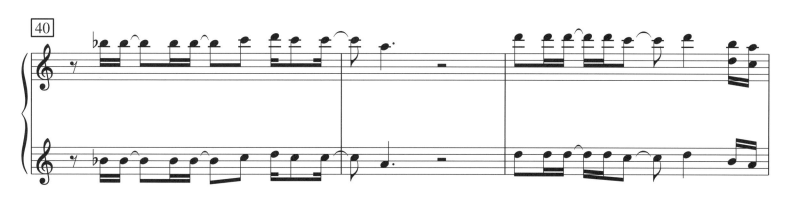

WHEN I'M SIXTY-FOUR

SECONDO

Words and Music by JOHN LENNON
and PAUL McCARTNEY

WHEN I'M SIXTY-FOUR

PRIMO

Words and Music by JOHN LENNON
and PAUL McCARTNEY

SECONDO

SECONDO

YESTERDAY

SECONDO

Words and Music by JOHN LENNON
and PAUL McCARTNEY

YESTERDAY

PRIMO

Words and Music by JOHN LENNON
and PAUL McCARTNEY

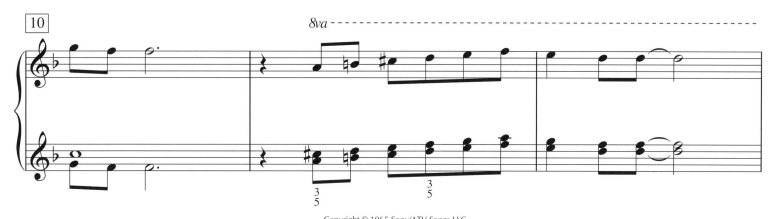

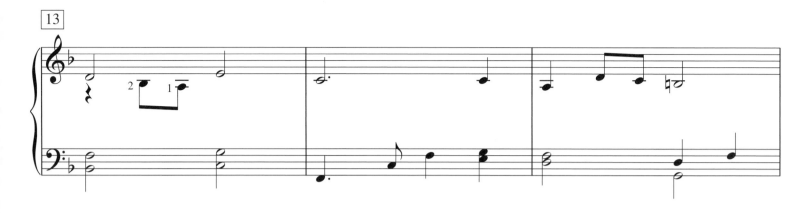

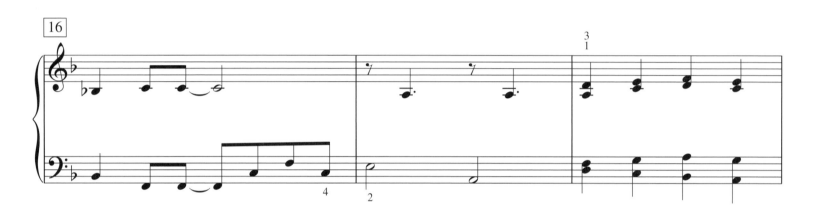

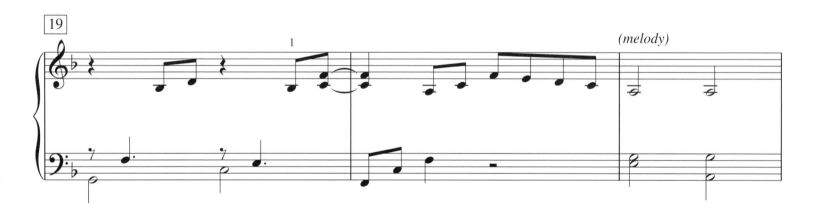

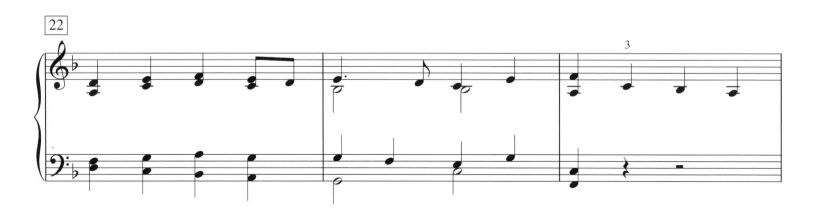

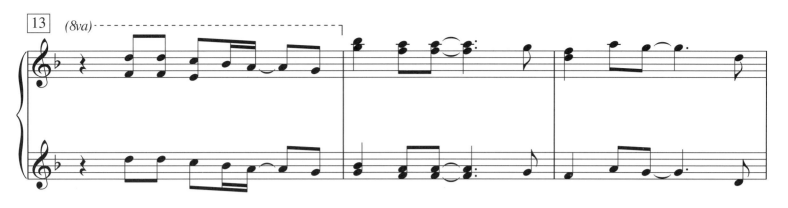

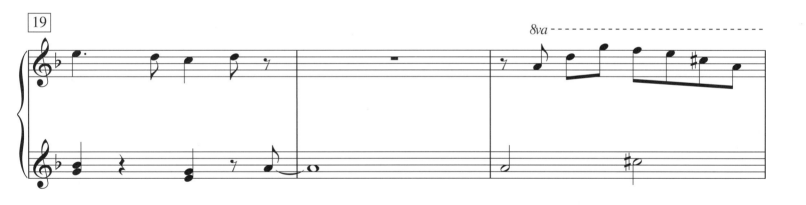

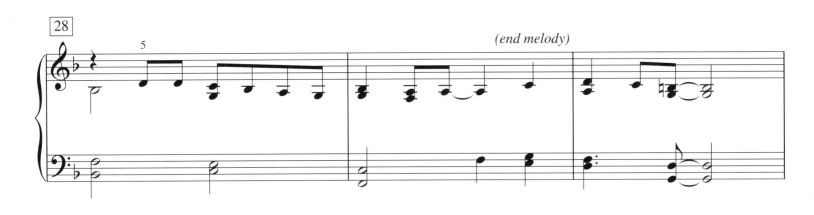

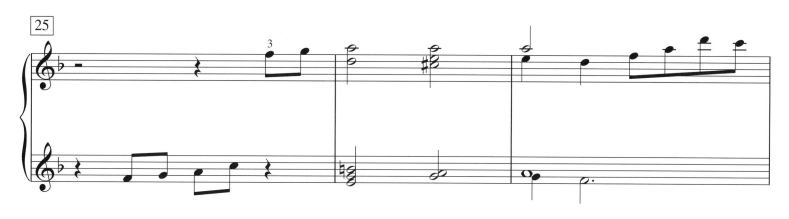

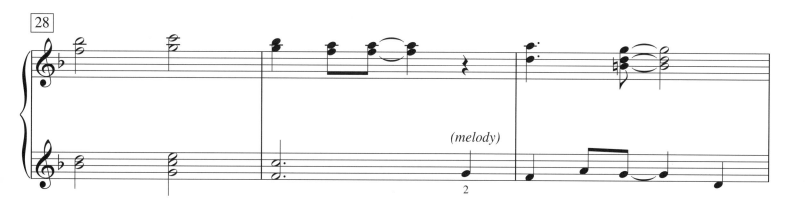

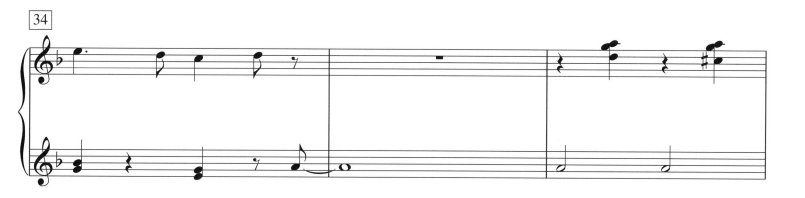

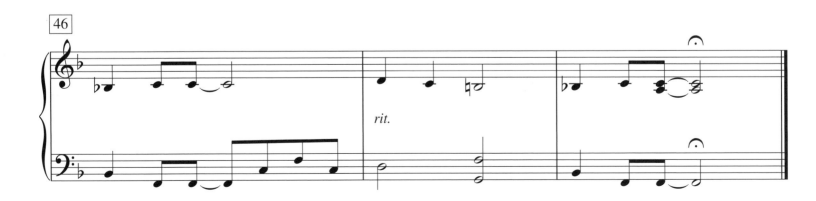

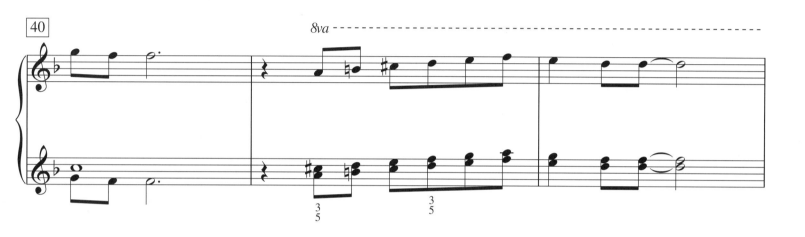

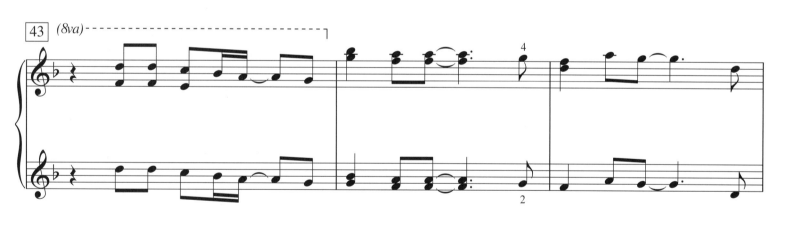

Piano for Two
A VARIETY OF PIANO DUETS FROM HAL LEONARD

ADELE FOR PIANO DUET

Eight of Adele's biggest hits arranged especially for intermediate piano duet! Featuring: Chasing Pavements • Hello • Make You Feel My Love • Rolling in the Deep • Set Fire to the Rain • Skyfall • Someone Like You • When We Were Young.

00172162.............................$14.99

CONTEMPORARY DISNEY DUETS

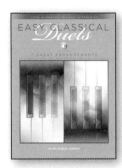

8 Disney piano duets to play and perform with a friend! Includes: Almost There • He's a Pirate • I See the Light • Let It Go • Married Life • That's How You Know • Touch the Sky • We Belong Together.

00128259 ....$12.99

BILLY JOEL FOR PIANO DUET

Includes 8 of the Piano Man's greatest hits. Perfect as recital encores, or just for fun! Titles: Just the Way You Are • The Longest Time • My Life • Piano Man • She's Always a Woman • Uptown Girl • and more.

00141139 ....$14.99

THE BEATLES PIANO DUETS – 2ND EDITION

Features 8 arrangements: Can't Buy Me Love • Eleanor Rigby • Hey Jude • Let It Be • Penny Lane • Something • When I'm Sixty-Four • Yesterday.

00290496.............................$15.99

EASY CLASSICAL DUETS

7 great piano duets to perform at a recital, play-for-fun, or sightread! Titles: By the Beautiful Blue Danube (Strauss) • Eine kleine Nachtmusik (Mozart) • Sleeping Beauty Waltz (Tchaikovsky) • and more.

00145767 Book/Online Audio $10.99

RHAPSODY IN BLUE FOR PIANO DUET

George Gershwin
Arranged by Brent Edstrom
This intimate adaptation delivers access to advancing pianists and provides an exciting musical collaboration and adventure!

00125150 ....$12.99

CHART HITS FOR EASY DUET

10 great early intermediate pop duets! Play with a friend or with the online audio: All of Me • Grenade • Happy • Hello • Just Give Me a Reason • Roar • Shake It Off • Stay • Stay with Me • Thinking Out Loud.

00159796 Book/Online Audio $12.99

THE SOUND OF MUSIC

9 arrangements from the movie/musical, including: Do-Re-Mi • Edelweiss • Maria • My Favorite Things • So Long, Farewell • The Sound of Music • and more.

00290389.............................$14.99

RIVER FLOWS IN YOU AND OTHER SONGS ARRANGED FOR PIANO DUET

10 great songs arranged for 1 piano, 4 hands, including the title song and: All of Me (Piano Guys) • Bella's Lullaby • Beyond • Chariots of Fire • Dawn • Forrest Gump - Main Title (Feather Theme) • Primavera • Somewhere in Time • Watermark.

00141055 ....$12.99

HAL LEONARD PIANO DUET PLAY-ALONG SERIES

This great series comes with audio that features separate tracks for the Primo and Secondo parts – perfect for practice and performance! Visit www.halleonard.com for a complete list of titles in the series!

COLDPLAY

Clocks • Paradise • The Scientist • A Sky Full of Stars • Speed of Sound • Trouble • Viva La Vida • Yellow.
00141054..............................$14.99

FROZEN

Do You Want to Build a Snowman? • Fixer Upper • For the First Time in Forever • In Summer • Let It Go • Love Is an Open Door • Reindeer(s) Are Better Than People.
00128260..............................$14.99

JAZZ STANDARDS

All the Things You Are • Bewitched • Cheek to Cheek • Don't Get Around Much Anymore • Georgia on My Mind • In the Mood • It's Only a Paper Moon • Satin Doll • The Way You Look Tonight.
00290577..............................$14.99

STAR WARS

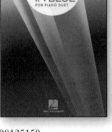

8 intergalactic arrangements of *Star Wars* themes for late intermediate to early advanced piano duet, including: Across the Stars • Cantina Band • Duel of the Fates • The Imperial March (Darth Vader's Theme) • Princess Leia's Theme • Star Wars (Main Theme) • The Throne Room (And End Title) • Yoda's Theme.

00119405..............................$14.99

HAL•LEONARD®
www.halleonard.com

ACOUSTIC PIANO BALLADS

16 acoustic piano favorites: Angel • Candle in the Wind • Don't Let the Sun Go Down on Me • Endless Love • Imagine • It's Too Late • Let It Be • Mandy • Ribbon in the Sky • Sailing • She's Got a Way • So Far Away • Tapestry • You Never Give Me Your Money • You've Got a Friend • Your Song.
00690351..$19.95

THE BEATLES KEYBOARD BOOK

23 Beatles favorites, including: All You Need Is Love • Back in the U.S.S.R. • Come Together • Get Back • Good Day Sunshine • Hey Jude • Lady Madonna • Let It Be • Lucy in the Sky with Diamonds • Ob-La-Di, Ob-La-Da • Oh! Darling • Penny Lane • Revolution • We Can Work It Out • With a Little Help from My Friends • and more.
00694827..$24.99

CLASSIC ROCK

35 all-time rock classics: Beth • Bloody Well Right • Changes • Cold as Ice • Come Sail Away • Don't Do Me like That • Hard to Handle • Heaven • Killer Queen • King of Pain • Layla • Light My Fire • Oye Como Va • Piano Man • Takin' Care of Business • Werewolves of London • and more.
00310940..$24.95

COLDPLAY

A dozen of the best from the British band: Amsterdam • Atlas • Clocks • Death and All His Friends • Fix You • For You • Paradise • The Scientist • A Sky Full of Stars • Speed of Sound • Violet Hill • Viva La Vida.
00141590..$19.99

DREAM THEATER – SELECTIONS FROM *THE ASTONISHING*

14 exact transcriptions: Dystopian Overture • The Gift of Music • Lord Nafaryus • Moment of Betrayal • My Last Farewell • Ravenskill • A Tempting Offer • When Your Time Has Come • and more.
00192244..$19.99

JAZZ

24 favorites from Bill Evans, Thelonious Monk, Oscar Peterson, Bud Powell, Art Tatum and more. Includes: Ain't Misbehavin' • April in Paris • Autumn in New York • Body and Soul • Freddie Freeloader • Giant Steps • My Funny Valentine • Satin Doll • Song for My Father • Stella by Starlight • and more.
00310941..$24.95

JAZZ STANDARDS

23 classics by 23 jazz masters, including: Blue Skies • Come Rain or Come Shine • Honeysuckle Rose • I Remember You • A Night in Tunisia • Stormy Weather (Keeps Rainin' All the Time) • Where or When • and more.
00311731..$22.95

THE BILLY JOEL KEYBOARD BOOK

16 mega-hits from the Piano Man himself: Allentown • And So It Goes • Honesty • Just the Way You Are • Movin' Out • My Life • New York State of Mind • Piano Man • Pressure • She's Got a Way • Tell Her About It • and more.
00694828..$22.99

BILLY JOEL FAVORITES

Here are 18 of the very best from Billy: Don't Ask Me Why • The Entertainer • 52nd Street • An Innocent Man • Lullabye (Goodnight, My Angel) • Only the Good Die Young • Say Goodbye to Hollywood • Vienna • and more.
00691060..$24.99

THE ELTON JOHN KEYBOARD BOOK

20 of Elton John's best songs: Bennie and the Jets • Candle in the Wind • Crocodile Rock • Daniel • Don't Let the Sun Go Down on Me • Goodbye Yellow Brick Road • I Guess That's Why They Call It the Blues • Little Jeannie • Rocket Man • Your Song • and more.
00694829..$24.99

ELTON JOHN FAVORITES

Here are Elton's keyboard parts for 20 top songs: Can You Feel the Love Tonight • I'm Still Standing • Indian Sunset • Levon • Madman Across the Water • Pinball Wizard • Sad Songs (Say So Much) • Saturday Night's Alright (For Fighting) • and more.
00691059..$22.99

KEYBOARD INSTRUMENTALS

22 songs transcribed exactly as you remember them, including: Alley Cat • Celestial Soda Pop • Green Onions • The Happy Organ • Last Date • Miami Vice • Outa-Space • Popcorn • Red River Rock • Tubular Bells • and more.
00109769..$19.99

ALICIA KEYS

Authentic piano and vocal transcriptions of 18 of her best-known songs, including: Fallin' • How Come You Don't Call Me • If I Ain't Got You • No One • Prelude to a Kiss • Wild Horses • A Woman's Worth • You Don't Know My Name • and more.
00307096..$22.99

THE CAROLE KING KEYBOARD BOOK

16 of King's greatest songs: Beautiful • Been to Canaan • Home Again • I Feel the Earth Move • It's Too Late • Jazzman • (You Make Me Feel) Like a Natural Woman • Nightingale • Smackwater Jack • So Far Away • Sweet Seasons • Tapestry • Way Over Yonder • Where You Lead • Will You Love Me Tomorrow • You've Got a Friend.
00690554..$21.99

JON LORD – KEYBOARDS & ORGAN ANTHOLOGY

14 from the Hammond organ pioneer, including: Burn • Child in Time • Fireball • Here I Go Again • Highway Star • Hush • Lazy • Perfect Strangers • Rubber Monkey • Smoke on the Water • Space Truckin' • Woman from Tokyo • and more.
00125865..$19.99

POP/ROCK

35 songs, including: Africa • Against All Odds • Axel F • Centerfold • Chariots of Fire • Cherish • Don't Let the Sun Go Down on Me • Drops of Jupiter (Tell Me) • Faithfully • It's Too Late • Just the Way You Are • Let It Be • Mandy • Sailing • Sweet Dreams Are Made of This • Walking in Memphis • and more.
00310939..$24.99

QUEEN

13 note-for-note transcriptions from the original recordings, including: Bohemian Rhapsody • Good Old-Fashioned Lover Boy • Killer Queen • Play the Game • Seven Seas of Rhye • Somebody to Love • We Are the Champions • You're My Best Friend • and more.
00141589..$19.99

ROCK HITS

30 smash hits transcribed precisely as they were played. Includes: Baba O'Riley • Bennie and the Jets • Carry On Wayward Son • Dreamer • Eye in the Sky • I Feel the Earth Move • Jump • Layla • Movin' Out (Anthony's Song) • Tempted • What a Fool Believes • You're My Best Friend • and more.
00311914 ....$24.99

ROCK KEYBOARD/ORGAN HITS

29 note-for-note transcriptions for keyboard/organ from the original recordings that made them famous: Born to Be Wild • Dirty Work • Gimme Some Lovin' • Highway Star • In-A-Gadda-Da-Vida • Like a Rolling Stone • and more.
00142488..$24.99

STEVIE WONDER

14 of Stevie's most popular songs: Boogie on Reggae Woman • Hey Love • Higher Ground • I Wish • Isn't She Lovely • Lately • Living for the City • Overjoyed • Ribbon in the Sky • Send One Your Love • Superstition • That Girl • You Are the Sunshine of My Life • You Haven't Done Nothin'.
00306698..$22.99

YOUR FAVORITE MUSIC
ARRANGED FOR PIANO SOLO

ADELE FOR PIANO SOLO – 2ND EDITION
This collection features 13 Adele favorites beautifully arranged for piano solo, including: Chasing Pavements • Hello • Rolling in the Deep • Set Fire to the Rain • Someone like You • Turning Tables • When We Were Young • and more.
00307585 ....$14.99

BATTLESTAR GALACTICA
by Bear McCreary
For this special collection, McCreary himself has translated the acclaimed orchestral score into fantastic solo piano arrangements at the intermediate to advanced level. Includes 19 selections in all, and as a bonus, simplified versions of "Roslin and Adama" and "Wander My Friends." Contains a note from McCreary, as well as a biography.
00313530 ....$17.99

THE BEST JAZZ PIANO SOLOS EVER
Over 300 pages of beautiful classic jazz piano solos featuring standards in any jazz artist's repertoire. Includes: Afternoon in Paris • Giant Steps • Moonlight in Vermont • Moten Swing • A Night in Tunisia • Night Train • On Green Dolphin Street • Song for My Father • West Coast Blues • Yardbird Suite • and more.
00312079 ....$19.99

CLASSICS WITH A TOUCH OF JAZZ
Arranged by Lee Evans
27 classical masterpieces arranged in a unique and accessible jazz style. Mr Evans also provides an audio recording of each piece. Titles include: Air from Suite No. 3 (Bach) • Barcarolle "June" (Tchaikovsky) • Pavane (Faure) • Piano Sonata No. 8 "Pathetique" (Beethoven) • Reverie (Debussy) • The Swan (Saint-Saens) • and more.
00151662 Book/Online Audio...$14.99

COLDPLAY FOR PIANO SOLO
Stellar solo arrangements of a dozen smash hits from Coldplay: Clocks • Fix You • In My Place • Lost! • Paradise • The Scientist • Speed of Sound • Trouble • Up in Flames • Viva La Vida • What If • Yellow.
00307637 ....$15.99

DISNEY SONGS
12 Disney favorites in beautiful piano solo arrangements, including: Bella Notte (This Is the Night) • Can I Have This Dance • Feed the Birds • He's a Tramp • I'm Late • The Medallion Calls • Once Upon a Dream • A Spoonful of Sugar • That's How You Know • We're All in This Together • You Are the Music in Me • You'll Be in My Heart (Pop Version).
00313527 ....$14.99

GREAT THEMES FOR PIANO SOLO
Nearly 30 rich arrangements of popular themes from movies and TV shows, including: Bella's Lullaby • Chariots of Fire • Cinema Paradiso • The Godfather (Love Theme) • Hawaii Five-O Theme • Theme from "Jaws" • Theme from "Jurassic Park" • Linus and Lucy • The Pink Panther • Twilight Zone Main Title • and more.
00312102 ....$14.99

PRIDE & PREJUDICE
12 piano pieces from the 2006 Oscar-nominated film, including: Another Dance • Darcy's Letter • Georgiana • Leaving Netherfield • Liz on Top of the World • Meryton Townhall • The Secret Life of Daydreams • Stars and Butterflies • and more.
00313327 ....$17.99

GEORGE GERSHWIN – RHAPSODY IN BLUE (ORIGINAL)
Alfred Publishing Co.
George Gershwin's own piano solo arrangement of his classic contemporary masterpiece for piano and orchestra. This masterful measure-for-measure two-hand adaptation of the complete modern concerto for piano and orchestra incorporates all orchestral parts and piano passages into two staves while retaining the clarity, sonority, and brilliance of the original.
00321589 ....$16.99

ROMANTIC FILM MUSIC
40 piano solo arrangements of beloved songs from the silver screen, including: Anyone at All • Come What May • Glory of Love • I See the Light • I Will Always Love You • Iris • It Had to Be You • Nobody Does It Better • She • Take My Breath Away (Love Theme) • A Thousand Years • Up Where We Belong • When You Love Someone • The Wind Beneath My Wings • and many more.
00122112 ....$17.99

STAR WARS: THE FORCE AWAKENS
Music from the soundtrack to the seventh installment of the Star Wars® franchise by John Williams is presented in this songbook, complete with artwork from the film throughout the whole book, including eight pages in full color! Titles include: The Scavenger • Rey Meets BB-8 • Rey's Theme • That Girl with the Staff • Finn's Confession • The Starkiller • March of the Resistance • Torn Apart • and more.
00154451 ....$17.99

TAYLOR SWIFT FOR PIANO SOLO – 2ND EDITION
This updated second edition features 15 of Taylor's biggest hits from her self-titled first album all the way through her pop breakthrough album, *1989*. Includes: Back to December • Blank Space • Fifteen • I Knew You Were Trouble • Love Story • Mean • Mine • Picture to Burn • Shake It Off • Teardrops on My Guitar • 22 • We Are Never Ever Getting Back Together • White Horse • Wildest Dreams • You Belong with Me.
00307375 ....$16.99

UP
Music by Michael Giacchino
Piano solo arrangements of 13 pieces from Pixar's mammoth animated hit: Carl Goes Up • It's Just a House • Kevin Beak'n • Married Life • Memories Can Weigh You Down • The Nickel Tour • Paradise Found • The Small Mailman Returns • The Spirit of Adventure • Stuff We Did • We're in the Club Now • and more, plus a special section of full-color artwork from the film!
00313471 ....$17.99

HAL•LEONARD®
7777 W. BLUEMOUND RD. P.O. BOX 13819 MILWAUKEE, WI 53213
www.halleonard.com

KEYBOARD *signature licks*®

These exceptional books and audio packs teach keyboardists the techniques and styles used by popular artists. Each folio breaks down the trademark riffs and licks used by these great performers.

  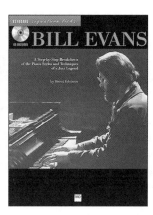 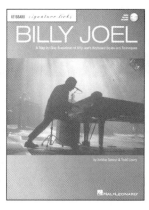 

THE BEATLES

20 Beatles classics: All You Need is Love • Back in the U.S.S.R. • Don't Let Me Down • Good Day Sunshine • Hello, Goodbye • Hey Jude • In My Life • Let It Be • The Long and Winding Road • Ob-La-Di, Ob-La-Da • Penny Lane • Revolution • She's a Woman • Strawberry Fields Forever • and more.
00329683 Book/Online Audio..$24.99

BEST OF BEBOP PIANO

by Gene Rizzo

16 classic tunes: April in Paris • Between the Devil and the Deep Blue Sea • Body and Soul • Cherokee (Indian Love Song) • East of the Sun (And West of the Moon) • I Don't Stand a Ghost of a Chance • If I Were a Bell • Lullaby of Birdland • On a Clear Day (You Can See Forever) • Prelude to a Kiss • Satin Doll • Thou Swell • and more.
00695734 Book/Online Audio..$19.95

BEST OF BLUES PIANO

by Todd Lowry

14 songs are covered: Big Chief (Professor Longhair) • Blueberry Hill (Fats Domino) • Cryin' in My Sleep (Jimmy Yancey) • Everyday I Have the Blues (Memphis Slim) • Honky Tonk Train Blues (Meade "Lux" Lewis) • The Pearls (Jelly Roll Morton) • Roll 'Em Pete (Pete Johnson) • Route 66 (Charles Brown) • Tipitina (Dr. John) • and more.
00695841 Book/Online Audio..$19.99

BILL EVANS

by Brent Edstrom

12 songs from this jazz legend: Five • One for Helen • The Opener • Peace Piece • Peri's Scope • Quiet Now • Re: Person I Knew • Time Remembered • Turn Out the Stars • Very Early • Waltz for Debby • 34 Skidoo.
00695714 Book/CD Pack..$22.99

BEST OF JAZZ PIANO

by Gene Rizzo

Includes 15 songs: Caravan • Come Rain or Come Shine • How Deep Is the Ocean (How High Is the Sky) • I'll Remember April • It's Only a Paper Moon • On a Clear Day (You Can See Forever) • Satin Doll • Stompin' at the Savoy • Take the "A" Train • There Is No Greater Love • Wrap Your Troubles in Dreams (And Dream Your Troubles Away) • and more.
00695763 Book/CD Pack..$22.99

BILLY JOEL

by Todd Lowry & Robbie Gennet

20 songs from the Piano Man: And So It Goes • Big Shot • The Entertainer • Honesty • Just the Way You Are • Lullabye (Goodnight, My Angel) • Movin' Out (Anthony's Song) • New York State of Mind • Piano Man • The River of Dreams • She's Always a Woman • She's Got a Way • Tell Her About It • Uptown Girl • more.
00345363 Book/Online Audio..$24.99

LENNON & McCARTNEY FAVORITES

by Todd Lowry

16 songs: Let It Be • Lucy in the Sky with Diamonds • Ob-La-Di, Ob-La-Da • Oh! Darling • Penny Lane • Rocky Raccoon • Strawberry Fields Forever • We Can Work It Out • With a Little Help from My Friends • The Word • You're Going to Lose That Girl • Your Mother Should Know • and more.
00695651 Book/CD Pack..$22.95

OSCAR PETERSON PLAYS STANDARDS

by Brent Edstrom

A dozen classics: All of Me • Between the Devil and the Deep Blue Sea • Falling in Love with Love • Fly Me to the Moon • Georgia on My Mind • I Love You • In a Mellow Tone • It's All Right with Me • It's Only a Paper Moon • My Heart Stood Still • On the Sunny Side of the Street • When Lights Are Low.
00695900 Book/Online Audio..$24.99

OSCAR PETERSON – CLASSIC TRIO PERFORMANCES

by Todd Lowry

14 of Oscar's trademark pieces: C-Jam Blues • Come Rain or Come Shine • Do Nothin' Till You Hear from Me • Don't Get Around Much Anymore • The Girl from Ipanema • I Got It Bad and That Ain't Good • The Lady Is a Tramp • My One and Only Love • Quiet Nights of Quiet Stars • Take the "A" Train • That Old Black Magic • and more.
00695871 Book/CD Pack..$22.99

BEST OF ROCK

by Todd Lowry

12 songs are analyzed in this volume: Cold as Ice (Foreigner) • Don't Do Me Like That (Tom Petty & The Heartbreakers) • Don't Let the Sun Go Down on Me (Elton John) • I'd Do Anything for Love (Meat Loaf) • Killer Queen (Queen) • Light My Fire (The Doors) • Separate Ways (Journey) • Werewolves of London (Warren Zevon) • and more.
00695751 Book/CD Pack..$19.95

BEST OF STEVIE WONDER

by Todd Lowry

14 of Stevie's best: Boogie on Reggae Woman • Don't You Worry 'Bout a Thing • I Just Called to Say I Love You • Living for the City • Master Blaster • My Cherie Amour • Overjoyed • Part Time Lover • Ribbon in the Sky • Send One Your Love • Sir Duke • Superstition • That Girl • You Are the Sunshine of My Life.
00695605 Book/CD Pack..$22.95

Prices, contents and availability subject to change without notice.

Visit Hal Leonard Online at
www.halleonard.com

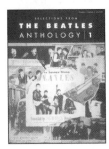

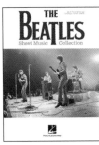